ALDO
LEOPOLD

ALDO LEOPOLD

American Ecologist

by
Peter Anderson

A First Book
Franklin Watts
A Division of Grolier Publishing
New York / London / Hong Kong / Sydney
Danbury, Connecticut

Cover photographs copyright ©: Townsend Dickinson/Comstock Inc;
University of Wisconsin, Madison, Archives (portrait)

Photographs copyright ©: University of Wisconsin, Madison, Archives: pp. 2 (X25-2643,
Robert McCabe), 24 (X25-2869, John D. Gutherie), 38 (X25-1937), 46 (X25-619), 50
(X25-2657), 55 ((X25-2870), 57 (X25-1307, Robert Oetking); Nina Leopold Bradley: pp. 8, 13,
18, 22, 25, 28, 39, 51, 54, 60; State Historical Society of Wisconsin: p. 10 (WHi(X3)30666);
The Lawrenceville School, John Dixon Library: p. 15; Forest History Society, Durham, N.C.,
U.S. Forest Service: pp. 19, 37; The Bettmann Archives: p. 30; National Agricultural Library,
Forest Service Photographic Collection: p. 31; Theodore Roosevelt Collection,
Harvard College Library: p. 35; Comstock: pp. 43 (Sharon Chester), 47 (George Lepp).

Library of Congress Cataloging-in-Publication Data

Anderson, Peter, 1956-
Aldo Leopold : American ecologist / by Peter Anderson.
p. cm. — (A First book)
Includes bibliographical references (p.) and index.
Summary: A biography of the ecologist whose pioneering contributions to wildlife management
have influenced generations of conservationists.
ISBN 0-531-20203-8
1. Leopold, Aldo, 1886-1948—Juvenile literature
2. Ecologists—United States—Biography—Juvenile literature.
3. Wildlife managers—United States—Biography—Juvenile literature.
4. Foresters—United States—Biography—Juvenile literature.
[1. Leopold, Aldo, 1886-1948. 2. Ecologists.]
I. Title. II. Series.
QH31.L618A73 1995
574.5'092—dc20
[B]   95-2596 CIP AC

CONTENTS

CHAPTER ONE
THE HUNTER'S APPRENTICE
7

CHAPTER TWO
THE NATURALIST'S ADVENTURES
12

CHAPTER THREE
FROM GREENHORN TO RANGER
17

CHAPTER FOUR
A CLOSE ENCOUNTER
27

CHAPTER FIVE
CALL OF THE WILD
34

CHAPTER SIX
IN THE EYES OF A WOLF
42

CHAPTER SEVEN
OUT AT THE SHACK
49

FOR FURTHER READING
61

INDEX
62

CHAPTER ONE

THE HUNTER'S APPRENTICE

One Saturday morning in the fall of 1900, Carl Leopold and his oldest son, Aldo, walked across town in the pre-dawn chill. Their softly spoken words clouded up and trailed away in the darkness. Two dogs followed, zigzagging through the empty streets.

At the depot, there was time for a quick breakfast—cold pork and beans, a couple of apples, and a cup of milk. Two twelve-cent tickets bought the hunters and their dogs a train ride across the Mississippi River to Illinois. There, they walked out along the big river to the wetlands where a swath of light rimmed the eastern sky. The rising sun revealed

Carl Leopold loved to hunt, but he never killed more
animals than he needed to feed his family.

ducks riding in on a cold north wind. Their wings flashed blue as they flew above the grassy bluffs that rose up out of the wetlands.

Such scenes may have been familiar to young Aldo, who often accompanied his father on weekend hunts, but there were always surprises. As he walked through the marsh, his attention drawn skyward by the great shifting Vs of migrating ducks, a mallard burst out of the rushes in front of him. Carl traced its flight with the barrel of his rifle. The gun blast echoed across the marsh. Aldo saw the duck's wings fold. The two dogs ran ahead to retrieve the fallen bird.

For Carl Leopold, each hunt was a way to participate in the natural cycle of life and death. One life given to feed another was nothing to be taken lightly. He was careful not to kill more than his family could use. Nor would he shoot those species that were becoming scarce.

He had seen enough bird migrations along the river to know that the great flocks were waning. Commercial hunters had killed and carted off wagonloads of game birds to supply markets and restaurants. Laws were needed to conserve the great flocks for future generations, and Carl would work hard to put those laws in place. In the meantime, he followed his own code of conservation rules and passed them onto Aldo.

While hunting and fishing with his father,
Aldo was introduced to the study of nature
and the practice of conservation.

In later years, Aldo would remember his father as a "pioneer of sportsmanship." He would recall the day his father had given him his first shotgun. "He said I might hunt partridges with it," Aldo wrote, "but that I might not shoot them from the trees. . . .

My dog was good at treeing partridge and to forego a shot in the tree in favor of a hopeless shot at a fleeing bird was my first exercise" in conservation. As Aldo learned to shoot a bird in flight, he came to realize that the rules that challenged him as a hunter also helped conserve bird populations.

Each day spent trekking through the marshes with his father taught young Aldo that there was much more to hunting than bringing home supper. Each outing beside the big river became a natural history lesson. A look inside a decaying log was a glimpse into the homes of mice and insects. Tracks and other signs revealed that a mink had killed a muskrat. Wild grape seeds seen in a pile of droppings told them what a raccoon was eating. Carl's keen awareness of the wetlands began to teach Aldo stories known only to those who could read the landscape.

THE NATURALIST'S ADVENTURES

Letters sent home from Lawrenceville Prep, a New Jersey boarding school where Aldo enrolled shortly after his seventeenth birthday, described his daily "tramps" across the snow-covered farmlands and forests surrounding the campus.

"I went north, across the country, about seven miles, and then circled back toward the west," he wrote on January 9, 1904, in his first report home. "Here every farm has a timber lot, sometimes fifteen or twenty acres, so it is a fine country for birds. It is about like Iowa high prairie, but the timber is more like the Michigan hardwood, the commonest trees

As a teenager, Aldo Leopold further developed his skills as a naturalist while attending prep school in Lawrenceville, New Jersey.

being oak, beech, ash, hickory, chestnut red cedar, and some elm."

Whenever he had an hour or two between classes, Aldo tramped off through the woods with a small pair of binoculars for looking at wildlife and a notebook in which to record his observations. Within a month, he had explored most of the terrain within a 10-mile (16-km) radius of campus.

He drew up his own maps, labeling the local land-marks with names like Big Woods, Fern Woods, Cat Woods, Owl Woods, Ash Swamp, the Boulders, Grove Country.

Even before he knew his classmates, Aldo knew the land. It wasn't long, however, before Aldo's daily adventures had earned him a reputation around campus. Often he was introduced as "the naturalist," a fitting title for someone who had always preferred solo time in nature to school socializing.

Soon, some of his fellow students began to wonder what Aldo found so interesting on his walks, and they began to tag along. A letter sent home in mid-March suggested that Aldo's love of walking the woods had caught on. It has "become a very general amusement . . . to tramp around the country with a staff and brag miles when returned home," Aldo wrote.

If Aldo's love of the outdoors had rubbed off on those who went tramping with him, perhaps his concerns for land and wildlife had too. One day, while out watching birds by a pond near campus, Aldo noticed a muskrat trying to swim out of a trap. He sprung the muskrat loose and continued on until he found another trap that contained a muskrat several weeks dead. Later, he found a third trap and a third muskrat, which had been killed several months earlier. Such careless trapping, as far as Aldo was con-

Students at the Lawrenceville school enjoyed learning about nature from Aldo, who at age seventeen was a budding naturalist.

cerned, should not go unpunished. "I have three traps on my hands," he told his parents in a letter, "which I will by no means give back to the person who traps . . . and . . . leaves the carcasses to rot."

Just as destructive was the draining of a campus pond. When they came upon the drained pond, Aldo and a friend waded out into the mud where they discovered thousands of wriggling minnows and tadpoles. "Why on earth they drain the pond I cannot imagine," he wrote home in a letter. "They do nothing to it but towards summer fill it up again." He intended to report the matter to the school headmaster. In the meantime he and a friend "procured some buckets and gathered each a dozen or so fish to keep and restock the pond" when it was filled again.

Such activities reflected Aldo's growing sense of responsibility toward wild places and the creatures that lived there. He had inherited his father's belief in conservation and he intended to put that belief to work by becoming a forester. Finishing his early education at a top-notch school such as Lawrenceville, he hoped, would prepare him to study forestry at Yale University.

CHAPTER THREE

FROM GREENHORN TO RANGER

Even after four long years of forestry school at Yale, and several ranger training sessions in Louisiana and Texas, Aldo Leopold couldn't help but feel like a "greenhorn" when he reported to his first job on the Apache National Forest in Arizona. It was all so new to him—this high, wide-skyed land, the tangy smell of sagebrush, tales told of grizzly bears.

There had been times at forestry school when Aldo had wondered if he had made the right choice. At Yale, he had given up his daily tramps in order to devote himself fully to the study of forestry. How strange it had seemed at

Aldo Leopold (front row, second from right)
poses with classmates at Yale University,
where he studied forestry.

In 1910, Aldo got acquainted with the Apache
National Forest on a horse named Jiminy Hicks.

times, to be cooped up in a library or classroom
pouring over numbers and charts to learn about
trees and forests.

Now, as he was issued his forest work clothes—
boots, leather chaps, and a hat big enough to camp out
under—all that was behind him. At a nearby ranch, he
saddled up a horse named Jiminy Hicks and received

his first roping lessons. Later, he was issued a set of pistols—standard equipment for traveling through country as wild and remote as was the Apache National Forest in 1909.

Aldo Leopold was among the first generation of foresters to graduate from the Pinchot Forestry School at Yale. Like Gifford Pinchot, America's pioneer forester who had established the school and now headed up the U.S. Forest Service, Aldo was dedicated to the caretaking of public lands. It was "more than work or a mere livelihood," Aldo wrote. It was "service and glorious service too."

Aldo's service on the Apache began with a month's worth of cross-country journeys on horseback, during which he inspected sawmills, marked timber sales, and met most of the rangers in the district. All wasn't work, however. Aldo found time to pull a few trout out of the local streams. And one day he rode Jiminy Hicks to the top of a mesa, where he looked out over waves of green forest, much of it yet to be officially surveyed.

Such surveys were the first step in the proper management of the western forests. Rangers were responsible for mapping their territory or "cruising the timber." Every two days a "cruiser" might cover as much as 3 square miles (7.8 sq km) of forest, recording the amount, location, and quality of all the timber.

After only a month with the Forest Service, Aldo was appointed to head up a crew of timber cruisers in the nearby Blue Range. Three months and 65,000 acres (26,000 ha) later, they would hobble into the district office having completed most of the work, but not without some difficulty. Aldo had made some mistakes on the surveying—he never had cared much for numbers. And some of the other cruisers had complained of his inexperience.

Nevertheless, Aldo had completed his initiation as a ranger, and he knew he had landed in the right profession. Someday, if all went well, he would supervise his own forest. "I was made to live on and work on my own land," he wrote his mother. "Whether it's a 100 acre farm or a 1,700,000 forest doesn't matter."

That opportunity would eventually come to Aldo, but not until he had faced more challenges as a forester. Unlike the Apache, Carson National Forest in northern New Mexico had been heavily abused. Since the 1850s, ranchers had been running increasing numbers of sheep and cattle on the forest without any rules to protect the land. By the time Aldo was appointed deputy supervisor of the Carson in the summer of 1911, large portions of the forest had been overgrazed and stripped of vegetation. Areas that were once grassy hillsides were now badly gullied.

**Some of the rangers at the Apache National Forest
(Aldo is in the front row, fifth from right)**

Without some decisive management of the forest, the next generation of ranchers would have little
left to graze their herds on. Previous forest supervi-
sors had done little to implement rules for grazing on
the forest land. It was up to Harry C. Hall, the new

supervisor, and Aldo Leopold, his young deputy, to change that. So Hall assigned each rancher a portion of the forest for their herds. He also set up rules to cut back on the size of sheep herds. These kinds of actions, he hoped, would help restore the range.

While many ranchers saw the need for cooperation to maintain the health of the forest, others resented the changes and threatened Hall and the other rangers. Hall retaliated with his own threats, but it was often up to Aldo to enforce the new grazing rules out on the range. To protect himself, Aldo kept his six-shooters close at hand.

As tense as the situation had become, Aldo was preoccupied with a different kind of showdown—a showdown of the heart. While visiting Santa Fe, Aldo had fallen in love with an attractive young schoolteacher named Estella Bergere. There had been other occasions for courtship in Aldo's life, but never a love this strong. The solitude, even isolation, of living in the forest only seemed to strengthen his feelings for Estella. When he heard that a young lawyer named Jamieson had proposed to marry Estella, Aldo knew it was time to take action.

On August 19, 1911, he took the train to Santa Fe so that he could deliver his own marriage proposal. Estella had known Aldo for only four months. Mostly they had shared their lives through letters, because

To keep public lands healthy for future generations,
foresters like Aldo Leopold helped enforce government
rules on logging and grazing.

**Aldo and Estella Leopold,
just after they were married in 1912**

Aldo was rarely able to get away from the forest. Still, she knew Aldo well enough to care for him, and she promised to make up her mind by November.

During the next few months, for Aldo the suspense was almost unbearable. "A sort of restless discontent is gnawing at me," he wrote to Estella. "I am not exactly on the right side of my nerves." Aldo's only relief came on Sundays when he was able to ride up into the surrounding aspen forests, which were ablaze with autumn colors. "I can hardly tell you what a blessed peace I find . . . in the hills," he wrote her. "I wouldn't be able to get along without them."

On November 10, when Aldo returned to Santa Fe, Estella said yes to their marriage, but her father wasn't as sure. He wanted time to find out more about Aldo's family background. It would be another week before he would approve of their wedding plans.

Aldo and Estella would be married the following October. In the meantime, Harry Hall decided to leave the Carson for a forest assignment in Oregon. Shortly after his twenty-fifth birthday, Aldo was chosen to replace his old boss as forest supervisor.

In the fall of 1912, Aldo and Estella began their lives together in the forest supervisor's house. Aldo stood on the front porch, puffing on his pipe and looking out over the Rio Grande Valley. Here, for a while anyway, he would have it all—his work, the land, and the woman he loved.

CHAPTER FOUR

A CLOSE ENCOUNTER

In April of 1913, Aldo was called away to another forest district to settle some disputes with local sheepmen. Even though he had been feeling slightly ill, Aldo rode the train over the Continental Divide and continued on horseback for five days. After ironing out differences with the sheepmen, he was on his way home when he was caught in a storm.

For two days, the rains came, along with periods of hail and snow that soaked his bedroll. Nights were long and cold. Aldo's energy reserves ran low. In his hurry to get home, Aldo decided to take a short cut across the Apache

As a young man, Aldo had enjoyed good health.
But in 1913, a spring storm and a serious disease
nearly took his life.

Reservation, but as darkness settled over the land, he realized he was lost.

The next day he would find the road back over the Divide, and he would ride until he could ride no longer. His legs had swollen up so severely that he had to slit open his boots to get them off. Fortunately, a stagecoach was able to deliver him to a doctor in a nearby town who diagnosed his problem as a bad case of rheumatism.

As it turned out, Aldo's sickness was more severe than that. By the time he rode up to his district ranger station on April 23, his face, hands, and arms had swollen up so badly that the other rangers hardly recognized him. Aldo insisted that the trip had gone well and that he felt just fine, but his fellow rangers knew better. They shipped him out on the next train to Santa Fe where he would arrive horribly swollen and barely alive.

Aldo's "rheumatism" turned out to be a serious kidney disease called nephritis. Had he not gone to Santa Fe, his sickness might have proved fatal. What he needed now was rest which, at that time, was the only known treatment for his disease.

But how long would it take to recover? After more than a year of rest, during which time Aldo took a leave of absence from the Forest Service, he was still unable to walk long distances. Under such circum-

By the beginning of the 1900s,
decades of unregulated hunting

and logging had taken a toll on American forests and
wildlife populations. As a conservationist, Aldo Leopold
sought out ways to save America's natural heritage
for future generations.

stances, the physical challenges of his old supervisor's job would have been too much. He couldn't help but wonder if he would ever regain his health.

In September 1914, Aldo, Estella, and their new-born son moved to Albuquerque, New Mexico, where Aldo accepted an office job at forest head-quarters. For a twenty-seven-year-old forester accustomed to a rugged life outdoors, such a job was not the one he would have chosen under ideal cir-cumstances. Nevertheless, after almost a year and a half recovering from his illness, he was grateful for any work at all. "Makes me feel pretty near like a U.S. Citizen again," he wrote in a letter to his father.

By 1915, Aldo's work assignments with the Forest Service began to reflect a growing public interest in wildlife and outdoor recreation. One of his projects was to write a wildlife management guidebook for rangers throughout the Southwest. For Aldo, this would involve gathering information on fish and game resources from the far corners of the forest.

It became clear, as Aldo gathered information for his wildlife management guide, that public sup-port was necessary for successful conservation efforts. Even though wildlife populations were pro-tected by state laws regulating hunting, these laws were often not enforced. Only public pressure could replace state game wardens who ignored hunting violations. And only public cooperation would enable the Forest Service to protect wildlife habitats in the forests.

To build that kind of cooperation, Aldo began speaking to citizen's groups and sportsmen's clubs throughout the state. He emphasized the need for hunting regulations and wildlife refuges. Conservation measures such as these, he insisted, were the best way to ensure a healthy future for wildlife in New Mexico.

CALL OF
THE WILD

Despite an increasingly active schedule, Aldo was still concerned about his own health. He had been told that a relapse of his sickness could occur if he pushed himself too hard. Such a relapse, the doctor said, would likely be fatal.

"To speak plainly, I do not know whether I have twenty days or twenty years ahead of me," he wrote in a letter to his Forest Service boss. "Whatever time I may have, I wish to accomplish something definite. Unless, however, I can settle down to one thing, I have small chance of such accomplishment. This 'one thing' is obviously game protection."

President Theodore Roosevelt (right) was famous for his love of the outdoors. The president praised Aldo Leopold for his devotion to wildlife conservation.

As uncertain as he may have been about his health, Aldo was sure of his direction. His early work for wildlife protection in New Mexico's forests had tapped into his deepest passions. His abilities to communicate and organize support had already helped establish game protection associations throughout the Southwest. A letter from President Theodore Roosevelt suggested that Aldo's work in New Mexico had set "an example to the whole country."

But for Aldo Leopold, this would be only the beginning. Just as Gifford Pinchot had recognized the need for forestry on American lands, Aldo had anticipated the need for wildlife management. In 1916, however, such a viewpoint was ahead of its time. It would be another ten years before Aldo would find a way to devote himself fully to the cause of wildlife conservation.

In the meantime, he would take on new responsibilities with the Forest Service. By 1919, only ten years after his first rangering job, Aldo was promoted to the second highest job in his region. In this job, he shared the responsibility for overseeing the management of more than 20 million acres (8 million ha) of forest. Among his accomplishments would be the creation of the nation's first wilderness area in the Gila National Forest in 1924.

In the 1910s and 1920s, Aldo worked to protect wildlife habitat in New Mexico's Gila National Forest.

In 1980, a portion of the Gila Wilderness
was renamed to honor Aldo Leopold.

Between 1910, when Aldo had first arrived in
New Mexico, and 1924, roads and other develop-
ments had carved up much of the Southwest's wild
lands. The Gila Wilderness was intended to protect
a portion of what remained. By prohibiting roads
and limiting other activities, the Forest Service
hoped to protect fragile soils, wildlife habitats, and
important water sources. The Gila Wilderness

By the mid-1920s, Aldo and his wife, Estella,
had four children. Here, Aldo holds his
newborn daughter, also named Estella.

would also provide a place for the kind of back-country adventure that Aldo described as one of the "necessaries of life."

If adventure was a "necessary of life" for Aldo, so was passion. Shortly before the Gila Wilderness was officially set aside in June 1924, Aldo left the southwestern lands that he loved to take a job at the U.S. Forest Products Laboratory in Madison, Wisconsin. As assistant director at the lab in Madison, he would be able to provide a comfortable home for his growing family—he now had four children. But the job would never bring him the satisfaction he was seeking. Wildlife, he realized, was his passion, not wood products.

Nevertheless, finding work related to wildlife in the 1920s was no easy task. Zoologists were few, and the field of wildlife management was unheard of. Still, Aldo could see a growing need for such work. At a national gathering of conservationists, he insisted that a wildlife management plan was needed for the entire country.

If anyone was qualified to take on such an enormous task, it was Aldo Leopold. His experience with wildlife management in the southwestern forests, along with his many speeches and writings on conservation, had earned him a widespread reputation. When a group of representatives from the sporting arms industry decided to fund a wildlife survey, they approached him with their proposal. If Aldo would oversee the project, they would put up the money for the kind of wildlife survey that he and others had been calling for.

Here was a chance for Aldo to combine his passion with his profession. For the next three years, he would study maps and records in libraries. He would talk with hundreds of farmers, scientists, and university professors. He would travel down the dusty roads that crisscrossed fields, forests, and farmlands, completing surveys of wildlife habitat in nine midwestern states.

If any one fact became clear from the results of the survey he published in 1931, it was that wildlife habitats—especially woodlots and wetlands—were disappearing. Bird species such as quail, prairie chicken, grouse, snipe, and woodcock were decreasing along with the habitats they depended upon.

As the years had passed, so had Aldo's worries about his own health. No longer did he fear the relapse that his doctors had warned him of. Now he was more concerned about the health of America's wildlife populations.

IN THE EYES OF A WOLF

Once, as a young ranger on the Apache National Forest, Aldo and his crew had paused on a canyon rim above the river to eat lunch. Below them something swam across the current. What appeared to be a deer from a distance turned out to be a wolf. As the wolf shook herself off on the riverbank, a half dozen wolf pups ran out of the nearby willows. They wrestled and tumbled over one another as they surrounded her in the meadow.

The men above wasted little time in reaching for their guns and firing into the wolf pack. "I was young then, and full of trigger itch," Aldo would

As a young man, Aldo's experience with a
dying wolf taught him that all creatures are
vital members of the natural community.

later write. "I thought that because fewer wolves meant more deer, that no wolves would mean hunter's paradise." In those days, most people felt that way. Because wolves and other predators were considered a threat to livestock and wild game species such as deer and elk, they were trapped and killed in large numbers.

By the time Aldo and the others had emptied their rifles from the rimrock above, the old wolf lay dying. One of the pups limped off into the rocks below. Aldo scrambled down the hillside, reaching the wolf shortly before she died. As he approached, the old wolf lashed out at him, and he saw in her eyes a fiery defiance that he would never forget. "I realized then, and have known ever since, that there was something new to me in those eyes," he later wrote, "something known only to her and the mountain."

What was it that the wolf and the mountain seemed to know? In later years, Aldo would come to realize that all species, including predators, were important members of the natural community. This was the wisdom that he would always associate with the eyes of that dying wolf.

Complex relationships among different species kept a natural community healthy. On the mountain, deer provided food for wolves and the wolves kept the deer population down. As long as there weren't too many deer browsing the hillsides, trees and shrubs would flourish. These trees and shrubs held soils in place which, in turn, enabled grasses to grow and helped to prevent erosion. "Ecology" was a term that scientists were just beginning to use for the study of community interactions such as these.

In 1933, when Aldo began to teach wildlife management at the University of Wisconsin, he introduced his students to ecology by asking them the kinds of questions that he often asked himself. How long had the landscape looked this way? What were the soils like? Why did certain trees grow in certain places? What kind of evidence was there for different wildlife species? Why were some species present while others were not? By posing such questions, he began to teach his students the language of the land.

The "professor," as his students called Aldo, was also sought out by state officials developing wildlife management strategies. Eventually, he would serve on the state wildlife commission, an agency that he had helped to establish in 1927. One of the most challenging issues facing the state wildlife commission had been the management of the deer population.

There were years when the population soared and deer starved in record numbers. All the leaves on the white cedar trees were stripped as high as the deer could reach. With little left to browse

To understand the ecology of a natural community, Aldo Leopold studied the plants and animals that lived there.

As a wildlife biologist, Aldo Leopold knew
that hunting was an important tool in the
management of deer populations.

on, the deer became so weak that they could be caught by hand.

To correct the situation, Aldo recommended a hunting season that would allow hunters to shoot does and bucks. (Usually, hunters were allowed to shoot bucks only.) He believed that wildlife refuges, normally off limits, should be temporarily open to hunters. Cancelling the usual bounty paid to hunters for wolf hides, he suggested, would help to decrease hunting of predators and increase their numbers.

Aldo knew that these measures would reduce deer populations and help restore their habitat. Still, there was heated opposition from those fearing that such a strategy would destroy the deer herd. To stand up to such criticism required a deep sense of confidence. Aldo relied on his ability to read the landscape. And he remembered what he'd seen in the eyes of a dying wolf.

CHAPTER SEVEN

OUT AT THE SHACK

With notebook and coffeepot in hand, Aldo walked out the door of "the shack," seated himself on a wooden bench that faced the morning star, and listened to a summer breeze brush through the leaves of an old elm tree. As a dog named Gus settled itself at his feet, Aldo took a cup from his shirt pocket and poured himself some coffee. A field sparrow began to sing.

Soon the robin that lived in the old elm tree chimed in. An indigo bunting claimed its territory on the branch of a dead oak. A tiny wren that nested in the eaves of the cabin added its voice to the chorus, followed by grosbeaks, thrashers, yellow warblers,

At "the shack," Aldo spent many days
studying the wildlife of Wisconsin.

Aldo and Estella Leopold with three of their children and their dog, Gus, at "the shack."

bluebirds, vireos, towhees, and cardinals. With so many performers on the stage, Aldo could no longer distinguish one song from another.

Soon the coffeepot was empty. The sun was on its way up. As Aldo closed his notebook, Gus bounded off through the dew-covered meadow. The scents that drifted past the dog's nose determined their route. On this particular July morning, they would saunter past great blue herons fishing down by the river. They would pass mother ducks herding their ducklings into the weeds. They would follow deer tracks that trailed off into the thickets.

As the bird chorus tapered off, Aldo would feel the sun warming his back. He would hear the distant clang of a cowbell. The faint rumble of a tractor engine would tell him that a neighboring farmer was beginning his day. By then, it was time to head home to "the shack" for breakfast.

"The shack" was actually a renovated chicken coop. It was the only building still standing on an abandoned farm north of Madison that Aldo first discovered in the winter of 1935. Aldo had so enjoyed hunting in the sand hills of Sauk County that he had been looking there for some land to buy. A friend who knew the area had driven him out to the orphaned farm beside the Wisconsin River.

They turned off a road near the river and walked up a two-rut trail underneath a row of wind-battered elm trees. Only sand burrs grew out of the farm's overworked soils, their brown stalks rising through the snow. A dug-out foundation was all that remained of the farmhouse that had once stood at the end of the tree-lined trail. The chicken coop was filled with a year's worth of manure.

Forlorn though it may have been, something about the abandoned farm charmed Aldo. Upon his return to Madison, he arranged for a lease of the property, which he later decided to buy. That spring, he would return to the sand-hill farm with his family. Along with his two sons, he would shovel the manure out of the old chicken coop and restore the roof. Affectionately known as "the shack," the renovated chicken coop would become the family's getaway.

But for Aldo, the abandoned farm would become much more than that. He had adopted this orphaned land and intended to restore it. Once the chicken coop had been renovated, Aldo and his family began to plant trees—several thousand each spring—along with wildflowers, ferns, and prairie grasses. Within ten years, the once desolate farm had become a budding tree plantation, attracting increasing numbers of wildlife species.

On his Wisconsin farm and elsewhere, Aldo recorded his observations of nature in notebooks and journals.

A Sand County Almanac

AND

SKETCHES HERE AND THERE

BY *Aldo Leopold*

Illustrated by CHARLES W. SCHWARTZ

NEW YORK

OXFORD UNIVERSITY PRESS 1949

Many of the essays that Aldo based on his studies of the natural world were later published in *A Sand County Almanac.*

For Aldo, the old farm became an outdoor laboratory where he could watch the landscape change. He began to record his observations on the farm: "River slightly up. Cool easterly breeze . . . Yellow foxtail had shed half its seed . . . Picked grapes for jelly. Still a few blackberries and dewberries. Chokecherries ripe . . . Squirrels beginning to work hickories near road cut. Nuts full size but shells still tight." Such careful attention to the details that made up nature's calendar continued to deepen his relationship with the land. The essays he soon began to write reflected that.

Aldo's love of land and wildlife had steered him into a variety of roles over the course of his life: naturalist, forester, wildlife manager, professor, and ecologist. On the farm, he felt a call to express himself as a writer. The essays that he began to write there and elsewhere would later be collected in a book called *A Sand County Almanac*.

In these essays, Aldo argued for the needs of the biotic or natural community that included soils, waters, plants, and animals, as well as humans. "A thing is right," he wrote, "when it tends to preserve the integrity, stability, and beauty of the biotic community. It is wrong when it tends otherwise."

This land ethic guided Aldo's efforts to restore the old farm by the Wisconsin River, an ongoing

Each spring, Aldo and his family
planted trees on their Wisconsin farm.

project that would occupy him for the rest of his life. He would spend his final days out at the shack planting pine trees with Estella and his daughter.

One day, they noticed the smoke blowing in from a neighboring farm. At first, Aldo wasn't concerned. He figured his neighbor was just burning down the stubble of a hay field. As the smoke continued to billow out toward the shack, Aldo sensed that it was more than that.

Aldo and his family gathered up brooms, buckets, shovels, a sprinkling can, and a fire pump, and drove off toward the smoke. As they drew closer, they could see a dozen of their neighbors trying to contain the blaze that had spread from a trash heap to the dried grass of the neighbor's farmyard, and beyond toward a marsh and a grove of pines on the Leopold's land.

It wasn't long before Aldo had taken charge of the situation, warning his neighbors not to get in front of the fire, and sending his daughter to another farmhouse to call the local fire department. Then he slung the fire pump over his shoulder and tried to dampen the ground along the edges of blaze.

On that April day in 1948, no one saw Aldo lie down in the grass after his heart attack. And no one saw the fire sweep lightly over his body. It wasn't until the fire department came and extinguished the blaze, that Aldo's body was discovered on the charred ground.

Just as Aldo Leopold had lived to defend the land and wildlife he loved, so too he had died. But the legacy Aldo left behind was as grand as the pines that continued to grow straight and tall on the family farm by the Wisconsin River. His environmental writings would influence generations of conservationists who followed trails that he had pioneered. He would be remembered as a forester, a wildlife manager, a professor, and an ecologist. He would be remembered as a man who knew the language of the land.

FOR FURTHER
READING

Amdur, Richard. *Wilderness Preservation*. New York: Chelsea House Publishers, 1993.

Challand, Helen J. *Vanishing Forests*. Chicago: Childrens Press, 1991.

DeStefano, Susan. *Theodore Roosevelt: Conservation President*. New York : Twenty-First Century Books, 1993.

Dunlap, Julie. *Aldo Leopold: Living with the Land*. New York: Twenty-First Century Books, 1993.

Faber, Doris. *Nature and the Environment*. New York: Scribner, 1991.

Hirsch, S. Carl. *Guardians of Tomorrow: Pioneers in Ecology*. New York: Viking Press, 1971.

Keene, Ann T. *Earthkeepers: Observers and Protectors of Nature*. New York: Oxford University Press, 1994.

Lorbiecki, Marybeth. *Of Things Natural, Wild, and Free: A Story about Aldo Leopold*. Minneapolis: Carolrhoda Books, 1993.

INDEX

Italicized page numbers
refer to illustrations.

Albuquerque, New Mexico,
    31
Apache National Forest, 16,
18, *18*, 19, 20, *21*, 41
Apache Reservation, 26–28
Arizona, 16

Bird population, 9, 40
Blue Range, 19

Carson National Forest, 20,
    25
Childhood, 7–15
Children, 31, *38*, 39, *50*, 52, 57
Continental Divide, 26
"Cruising the timber," 19–20

Death, 57–58
Deer population, 43, 44–47

Ecology, 41–44, 55, 58
Education, 11–16

Forestry, 15, 16–25, 35, 41, 55,
    58

Forest Service, U.S., 19, 28, 31,
    32, 33, 35, 37

Game protection, 9, 33, 35.
    See also Wildlife
        management
Game protection associations,
    35
Gila National Forest, 35, *36*
Gila Wilderness area, 35–39, *37*

Hall, Harry C., 21, 22, 25
Health, 26–31, 33, 34, 40
Hunting, 7–10, *29*, 31, 43
Hunting regulations, 31, 32, 47.
    See also Wildlife
        management
Hunting seasons, 47

Illinois, 11
Iowa, 11

Jiminy Hicks, 18, *18*, 19

Lawrenceville Prep, 11, *14*, 15
Leopold, Aldo, *10*, *12*, 17, *18*,
    21, *23*, *24*, 27, *45*, *50*, 56
        as ecologist, 41–44, 55,
        58

as forester, 16–25, 55, 58
as teacher, 44, 55
as wildlife manager,
    35–39, 55, 58
as writer, 31–32, 39–40,
    54, 55
Leopold, Carl (father), 7–10,
    8, 13, 15, 31
Leopold, Estella Bergere (wife),
    22–25, *24*, 31, *50*, 57
Leopold, Estella (daughter), *38*
Louisiana, 16

Madison, Wisconsin, 39, 51, 52
Marriage, 22–25
Michigan, 11
Mississippi River, *7*

Nephritis, 28
New Mexico, 20, 32, 34, 35, *36*

Oregon, 25

Pinchot, Gifford, 19, 35
Pinchot Forestry School, 19

Rheumatism, 28
Rio Grande Valley, 25
Roosevelt, Theodore, *34*, 35

Sand County, Wisconsin, 53, 54

Sand County Almanac, A, *54*, 55
Santa Fe, New Mexico, 22,
    25, 28
Sauk County, Wisconsin, 51
Shack, the, 48–58, *49*, *50*
Sporting arms industry, 39

Texas, 16
Trapping, 13–14

United States Forest
    Products Laboratory, 39
University of Wisconsin, 44

Wilderness areas, 35–39
Wildlife management, 31–32,
    34, 35, 39, 44, 55, 58.
    See also Game protection,
    Hunting regulation
Wildlife management
    guidebook, 31–32
Wildlife refuges, 32, 47
Wildlife survey, 39–40
Wisconsin, *49*
Wisconsin River, 51, 55, 58
Wolves, 41–43, *42*, 47

Yale University, 15, 16, *17*, 19

Zoologists, 39

ABOUT THE AUTHOR

Peter Anderson has worked as a river guide, carpenter, newspaper reporter, writing teacher, editor, and wilderness ranger. He has written ten books for young readers on topics related to nature, Native Americans, and the history of the American West. Currently, he lives in Salt Lake City, Utah.